T0069147

Colander

Books by Michael McFee

Poetry:

To See (with photographer Elizabeth Matheson)
Sad Girl Sitting on a Running Board
Vanishing Acts
Plain Air

Anthology:

*The Language They Speak Is Things to Eat: Poems by Fifteen
    Contemporary North Carolina Poets*

Colander

Poems by

Michael McFee

Carnegie Mellon University Press
Pittsburgh 1996

Acknowledgments

Thanks to these magazines, their editors and readers, for first publishing these poems:

Poetry: "Paper," "Answering Machine," "Grave Grass," "Clotheslines," "Multi-purpose Protractor," "Scanning the Poetry Shelves in Heaven," "Champagne," "The All-Dog Siren Choir," "The Bat," "Pas de Deux"

Appalachee Quarterly: "The Tunnel," "Spirit Paper"

The Atlantic: "Buzzard"

Virginia Quarterly Review: "Barnum's Animal Crackers," "Old Baseball Found under a Bush," "Colander"

Charlotte Poetry Review: "The Elevators," "Performance," "Shoulder"

Cellar Door Biweekly: "Change"

Tar River Poetry: "Nap," "Paradise"

Shenandoah: "Pencil"

Hudson Review: "To a Muse"

Light Year '86: "In Medias Res"

Kenyon Review: "Politics," "The Roof Men"

Southern Poetry Review: "Address Book"

Harvard Magazine: "Ice Cube"

The News and Observer: "Cancer"

Greensboro Review: "Linville Caverns"

The Nation: "When I Read to My Son"

DoubleTake: "My Aunt Smokes Another Lucky"

Carolina Quarterly: "Pearly Gates"

Thanks also to: the Durham Arts Council, Incorporated, for a seasonal grant; Frances Coombs, for input; and Michael Chitwood and Robert Morgan, for friendship and good advice.

Publication of this book is supported by grants from the National Endowment for the Arts in Washington, D.C., a Federal Agency, and from the Pennsylvania Council on the Arts.

Contents

for Scott Byrd,
writer's reader, generous friend

I

Paper

I write on the fingers and fractions of fingers
my Uncle Slim lost to the Champion machines.

I write on the Fiberville duplex by the Pigeon
where he and his wife raised a skinny family.

I write on that lethal river, its downstream liquor
snaking like venom all the way to Tennessee.

I write on the stench seeping up the valleys,
the first thing smelled each morning, hours away.

I write on the bitter laugh of my aunt, who said,
"Oh, you get used to the smell after a while."

I write on the smoke of my uncle's cigarette
clutched between stubs on his huge right hand.

I write on my father's father, killed at the mill
in an accident nobody alive can quite remember.

I write on that smoldering mill, a set for Hell,
its mountains of pulp and infinitesimal men.

I write on blood, on clear-cut, on a watermark
lost to light. I write on transfigured paper.

The Tunnel

The rain would hold its breath
as we hissed into the tunnel, its exhilarating gloom,
dad snapping the lights on
and slowing way down to see if my sister and I could
hold our breath to the distant
arch of light, my mother scolding him for teasing us,
my sister flailing the seat
as she honestly hoarded her air like a penny-diver
and I cheated again, stealing
oxygen through my nose but bulging my cheeks and eyes
in mock asphyxiation, always
waiting till we burst the drumskin of rain and day
and my sister had collapsed
gasping like a landed fish on the floorboard to finally
spout the astonishing breath
out of my false body, always my father's boy, always.

Answering Machine

Mother

She always hated it, would hang up in disgust
or start talking before I stopped talking,
the shadow of her twang lingering like smoke
before the beep. So I play back this old cassette
hoping for a scrap of her voice, some syllables
I can splice to her legacy of snapshots
as a kind of soundtrack to a kind of movie,
a filmstrip life that signals between frames.
But it's been too many years, she's been erased
by spoken postcards, junk mail, dates and time
I'll never need again, blank static stretches
as the tape reels in its slick magnetic tongue.

Father

He hated it too, but had plenty of time to wait
and try to swallow the quavery widower's voice
that lodged in his throat right after she died.
But nothing helped, he always sounded morose,
even the most casual message verged on tears,
something about this unanswering machine
made his loneliness worse. It was like talking
to God in the dark, Him taping every sad prayer.
Or talking to her, all the unresponsive day.

Others

It's like listening to a high-school yearbook,
so many friends and others saying, Keep in touch!
I even hear my out-of-town self: how peculiar
my absent voice sounds, addressing its absence!
But my dead parents don't surface, no matter
how deep I angle for their voices, not even
when I turn the volume to MAX during silences.

Then, at the tape's dead end, I hear myself
cut in on a message and say, "Hello? Hello?
I'm here, I just walked in." There's a pause,
the steady exhale of the long-distance line,
the ambient noise of chatter and electricity,
then I speak again: "Hello? Dad? Is that you?"
"Are you there son?" he asks, as the tape runs out.

Grave Grass

What a bad implant, this gravelly sod
shovelled before the grave was dug
then quickly stamped back into place,

a clumsy grass puzzle with clay seams.

The scar tissue of our parents' plot
never quite heals: no matter
how often or seldom we come to tend it

we always feel the unsettling welt

of their caskets in the wounded ground,
kneeling to steady ourselves and to pluck
metastatic chickweed from their names

next to the level easement they bought for us.

Clotheslines

The lines sag deeper and deeper with sweet wet gossip.
The clever pins do headstands all day, jaws clenched.

My parents preached the virtues of clothes dried outside.
Dryers are a rich man's fad, the static can kill you.

A Halloween of underwear, haunting the neighborhood.
The socks' threadbare parody of Christmas morning.

The shirts surrender, they pray, they are crucified.
The hung pants stiffen like casts in the hungry sun.

I press out their rigor mortis with Gothic devotion.
I polish the clothes with the day's lost water and heat.

My parents were well-dressed the last time I saw them.
The basket feels fuller and lighter as I walk back in.

Haunt

My father haunts me
from within. At first it's cosmetic,
          a few gray highlights
seeping into my moustache and hair:
          the mirror calls it
distinguished, after all I'm an adult.
          But then I hear him
insinuating his fateful undertone
          whenever I speak,
his self-pity stiffening my joints,
          troubling my stomach
as his was troubled. I can feel him
          dimming every sense
until I realize that nothing will
          exorcise my dad,
who means to stay until he's claimed
          every thankless cell
inside. He's in there making himself
          right at home, smoking
cigarettes, drinking coke. *Oh my aching*
          sacroliliac!
he cries down the unsettling hall
          of the house he made,
that unmade him, that he is now unmaking.

II

Buzzard

Circuit rider, the methodist
of carrion. Undertaker
of fate, the day's data. Black soul
hungering for a body. God
wobbling above, missing nothing.

Barnum's Animal Crackers

The animals have been trapped for generations
in this sunny caravan with four flat wheels.
No matter how well the cub pedals his unicycle
while juggling, Barnum never opens the doors

on his ark. There he is on the roof, barking
through a bloody megaphone, calling us to behold
beasts of jungle and tundra, forest and veldt
and ocean, this priceless menagerie of the exotic,

step right up, there's a cracker born every minute!
The antelope and camel look blasé, the walrus
startled in his second-story cell with no water.
Alligator and panther bare keen teeth, as trained.

And that's not all, folks, there's much more!
barks Barnum's dapper twin. Just roll back the top
and taste the peaceable kingdom preserved inside,
the lion and the lamb recumbent with the leopard,

the delectable heads and tails of quadrupeds
that might be rhinos or bears, it's hard to tell
when the cookie's crumbled like a sandstone tablet—
but it doesn't matter, they all taste so sweet!

And now we know why the animals look so sullen
in this flimsy purse we can swing on a string,
in this block we can eat like fairy-tale termites,
in this portable cardboard altar of extinction:

they know that their only escape is through us,
these gods we melt on our disbelieving tongues
as the calliope whistles and the long whips snap
and the pawpads measure the edge of the cage again.

The Elevators

1

The elevators in their lonely shafts
call to each other like woodcocks courting—
peent peent peent, as Peterson mimics
in his field guide nested on the 7th floor.

Their echoes fill the shafts as they rise
and call and fall and rise and call again.

2

The elevators discharge readers like miners
into the dangerous tunnels of words.
Ideas light their hardhats, showing the way.

3

The elevators are tight proscenium stages,
every stop a curtain call.
But where are the flowers, the *bravos* and *encores*?
And where are the wings to exit, blowing kisses?

The one way out is through the restless audience.

4

The elevators feel like coffins when you're stuck,
buried alive, rationing your precious breath.
Remember that horror movie where the walls
kept closing in, crushing the helpless hero?
Remember Lazarus, stumbling back into the light?

5

The elevators are a nightmare's dream:

you stick out your arm to stop the door
and it amputates you at the elbow,

or the door opens onto a 13th floor
and you step into that glorious hologram
and sink through it like a cloud,

or the elevator stalls and you pick up the phone
only to hear God, or Satan in the basement,
or Elisha Otis welcoming you to the afterlife,
the tallest skyscraper ever constructed.

6

The elevators of glass in the fancy hotels
were designed by voyeurs for exhibitionists,
or vice versa. How can you ever sneak a kiss?

7

The elevators tire of sociology students
riding them all day like giddy kids,
mapping the predictable strategies
of attraction, avoidance, personal space,

all eyes lifted toward the scale of light.

8

The elevators can't stop thinking of numbers.
They will never count themselves to sleep.

9

The elevators are closets that the clothes
can walk out of, and the jackets and hats,
and all the paired shoes waiting on the floor.

10

The elevators are actually claustrophobic.
They hate to be crammed with people even more
than people hate to be crammed onto them.

They want to wait wide open in the lobby
all night, utterly empty, filled with shadows.

11

The elevators in downtown office buildings
were operated by old men on stools
who asked your floor and then pulled shut
glass panel doors and a brass folding screen,

dialing your number on a big gold wheel
that looked like something from a submarine,
whistling as you rose past white numbers
stencilled at the base of every stop

then easing the elevator into place,
adjusting the car up or down until its floor
matched the building's and they could draw back
the heavy screen and doors and sing out,

"Watch your step, now." And hit the spittoon
with a bullseye of tobacco as you walked away.

12

The elevators have slow shutters, allowing
just enough light into the camera.

Something always develops between floors.

In the pause as the doors slowly open,
you are the finished picture, perfectly framed.

14

The elevators are not triskaidekaphobic.

Change

Dead presidents
caucus in my pocket.

They strike stiff
profiles in the light,

pious cameos
nobody really wants.

But in the immortal
liberty of dark

they change:
they shuck their grim

wigs and halos,
they sweet-talk machines

out of everything,
they tell bad jokes

and laugh loudest
when I'm most nervous,

ghosts of money,
belling me.

Nap

Little deep word, how we crave
a dip in your healing waters!

Nap was once the ocean where we lived,
surfacing occasionally.
Now it's just a shrunken pool,
part of an oasis in the Desert of Light.

You won't find it on any map:
it requires a long unrouted detour
through Lesser Amnesia,
a hiatus in the mind's greedy itinerary.

But cats know where it is, and dogs,
and old men in the shade catching forty winks
so delicious they will always wake
salivating, born again.

Multi-purpose Protractor

It took the measure of the world, and more,
this cheap plastic template
I packed to school in my United States pencil box.

What bored draftsman first imagined
such an unlikely tool, its suggestive French curve
and angles, its circle gauge like blown bubbles,
and at the center of this reverie
the protractor itself, a perfect half-risen sun
with 180 imploding black rays?

On blank straightedge mornings
I'd slip it from my box with a hypodermic pencil
and rule a fantastic geometry,

something a lot better than the classroom
with its cemetery of desks,
or the country I could eclipse with my hand,
or the world that stayed rolled up over the blackboard.

Pencil

Seven-inch standard the shrink fingers
as he asks about my sex life,
the lead in my pencil . . .

There is no lead in pencils anymore.

But maybe he's speaking in a manner of speaking
since *pencil* does derive from *pencillum*
which is itself a diminutive
of *penis*, tail.

Or maybe he knows a hand completes a pencil
as a pencil completes a hand,
the focus of its fingers, its ideal digit,

shaft to the point of sketchy words or lines,
the arrow of provisional thought.

•

Carpetbaggers saw pencils
in red cedar that survived the war intact—
fence posts, rails, log cabins, barns.

They bought the wood and shipped it north
to factories, then shipped the finished product
back south where no one could afford it.

Every Confederate obelisk is a pencil
writing *remember* on a Union sky,

and every pencil is an obelisk
branded with exotic gilt inscriptions—
Venus, Koh-i-noor, Blackfeet, Eagle, Ticonderoga,
Your Message Here.

●

Even the smoothest sheet
is sandpaper to fresh graphite points,
a file shearing off shavings,

a perfect excuse for the procrastinator
to grind pencils into sharpeners
until he has a fistful of bayonets
ready for the enemy,

until their tips snap under pressure
and he must rise to sharpen them again.

He tattoos each pencil's facets
with teethmarks, as if his bite could bear
words from the mouth to the page.

●

Graded yourself, you graded us.
We broke the big test's seal with your eraser,
riddled a standardized form with black holes
dug by a nervous #2,

prayed the key would somehow fit our guesses.

When you hit the floor, it was music,
a brief drum roll
that restored the bloody marrow to our bones.

●

You are made to be destroyed,
worn to a mortal stub
from rubber crown to always-broken heel.

Your drafts will smudge or fade or be erased
or finally legally inked over.

And yet how jaunty you look
tucked behind the ear, like a bright idea
on the verge of exclamation!

●

Aromatic candle
whose black wick I slowly burn,

your color is healthy caution,
your shape is home,

a cell
from the infinite hive of words.

III

Scanning the Poetry Shelves in Heaven

Not fat
       pulpy handfuls of fiction,
but this:
       slim volumes, tightly stratified,

each book
       thinner than a curious fingertip,
so light
       it's like mica in the palm,

each line
       a miracle of lamination
so subtle
       your nail can't discover the seam,

each word
       an irreducible lucent fleck
so stubborn
       you can't quite scrub it from your skin.

To a Muse

You look like an old-fashioned microphone,
your mesh stained with the breath

of several thousand cups of tea
since my wife found you at Woolie's in Cambridge

years ago. Late in the morning
or afternoon, whenever inspiration cools,

I hook you to a mug, ease a heaping teaspoonful
of Twinings into your basket,

English, Irish, Prince of Wales, Ceylon, Souchong,
politics are a meaningless brew,

and wait for the perfect steep
as I wait for a phrase, lifting you from the water

at just the right ripeness. O Astex Strainer,
you are a homely muse

with your melted handle and second-degree burns,
with the caffeine-taint I could try

to scratch from your stiff lip
but don't, knowing that it corresponds somehow

to the tarnish my teeth and cup
have taken from you, your lasting tannic kiss.

And when my boiling invocations finally exhaust
your patience, I will retire you

to a place of honor on my desk
where I can lift you to my face when lost in thought

like a mask whose subtle fumes
help the body remember what the mind keeps forgetting.

Old Baseball Found under a Bush

On this ultimate spitball
        steeped for who knows how many unseasonable seasons
           under a parkside bush,

two tiny snails are tracing
        fingerings: fast ball, slider, split finger, curve,
           a methodical rehearsal

over horsehide so putrefied
        the regulation pressure-wound muscular core beneath
           is dissolving like newsprint.

This is something you want
        to drop, not throw: the old flirtation with gravity
           has gone sour, there's too much

dirt and sweaty scuff and smell,
        the once-delicate swell of the never-ending stitches
           hidden in the pitcher's grip

protrudes like bones through skin.
        This thing was meant for the heavy hands of the dead.
        So I bury it under some leaves

as the snails polish their trail,
        a couple of umpires searching for whatever it was
           that made this ball jump once.

Baseball Fields Seen from the Air

In the absolute panic of landing,
these are the best of all possible signs.

Their sandy fans unfold below.
Home is the hub of that sweet green breeze.

Pie in the sky, pie of the irrefutable earth!
Each field is a thick delicious slice.

A little league park that's a red-clay scar,
a minor league field with mange,

a major league stadium's emerald diamond
set in a golden scallop shell—

they all broadcast the same welcome message,
V for victory, peace be with you.

What crop could grow in such peculiar fields?
What silt-rich rivers left such deltas?

The plane's loud shadow haunts the waiting game.
There's a sudden sound that will release us.

Each field is a clock where time has stopped,
fair hands frozen at the quarter hour.

Paradise

We arrive by shuttle bus, precious tickets
    clenched in our pockets, the stadium gleaming
like a setting for heaven's vast sapphire.

For ages, we have been focusing our desire:
    the city, its rich skyline a mirage that grew
but didn't fade away; the park; and finally

the field, this bullseye, Adam the caretaker's
    brilliant crosshatching of outfield grass,
his cunning draftsmanship of basepath dirt,

his masterpiece the mound, a holy mountain
    whose summit is commanded by the angel
starting for our home team, his first pitch

a quick strike triggering a deafening bloom
    of flashbulbs. The game is still written
in code, a flurry of signs, but here, at last,

we understand the furtive catcher, the coaches
    whose hands speak in tongues, the banners
strung from the upper deck, the blimp overhead

flashing its helpful messages. And we can see
    God nod in his private box, the president
and his stiff wife trying hard to wake Him up

by smiling harder than ever. And so we laugh
        and pound our bruised hands and shout sounds
until the roar is so loud we can't hear ourselves

and the game achieves its final focus: the ball,
        arcing from a remote bat straight at us, over
the centerfielder's black glove, over the fence

whose thin blue line separates win from loss,
        into the dry moat behind the outfield wall
that we fill with our cries of joyful disbelief.

Champagne

What was that French monk thinking
when he sealed the Renaissance in a bottle?

The flute whose crystal is a frozen breath,
the airy liquid or liquid air
that barely seems like drinking anything—
this is the marriage of all states of matter,
its quintessence lifted to our lips.

There is much danger in such buoyance:
the pressure can blind you.

And such brilliance must be hidden
in deep darkness for many years to mature,
in labyrinthine tunnels filled
with bottles as thick and dark and heavy
as champagne is not.

This queen must keep her crown wired on.
Look at the glorious bubble-grapes ascending!

Dom Pérignon, are you the hangover moon
lingering in the afternoon sky
as our party starts to clean the yard
littered with corks like toppled mushrooms?
The sound of their launching made quite a salvo.

Cheers! we kept shouting, toasting everything,
sipping the effervescent sky all night.

Spirit Paper

When I die, spread a ream
of 100% cotton bond
at the bottom of my grave
and set it on fire,

for all the poems I never
got around to writing,
for all the poems I wrote
but just wrote wrong.

Say a prayer for forgiveness
to all decomposed poets,
then lower my coffin, slowly,
onto the restless ashes.

IV

In Medias Res

His waist,
like the plot,
thickens, wedding
pants now breathtaking,
belt no longer the cinch
it once was, belly's cambium
expanding to match each birthday,
his body a wad of anonymous tissue
swung in the same centrifuge of years
that separates a house from its foundation,
undermining sidewalks grim with joggers
and loose-filled graves and families
and stars collapsing on themselves,
no preservation society capable
of plugging entropy's dike,
under the zipper's sneer
a belly hibernation-
soft, ready for
the kill.

Politics

The chairman is washing his dirty hands again
and I am trapped here in the handicapped stall
as he palms a thin red liquid from the dispenser,
looking in the mirror at my shackled ankles.

And I am trapped here in the handicapped stall
while he works up a massive lather on his arms,
looking in the mirror at my shackled ankles,
wondering how long I can loiter on the toilet

while he works up a massive lather on his arms
and patiently rinses them in the gagging sink,
wondering how long I can loiter on the toilet.
The chairman brushes his fresh-bleached teeth

and patiently rinses them in the gagging sink.
How long can I sit here and feign this crap?
The chairman brushes his fresh-bleached teeth,
lets me gather enough paper to hang myself.

How long can I sit here and feign this crap?
He admires himself in the stainless fixtures,
lets me gather enough paper to hang myself.
As the chairman arranges his expensive hair

he admires himself in the stainless fixtures,
my fate is measured by his comb's dismal hiss.
As the chairman arranges his expensive hair
the fluorescent tubes wave a pale farewell,

my fate is measured by his comb's dismal hiss,
the tiles are an emptied graph of my life.
The fluorescent tubes wave a pale farewell:
I must peel myself from this cracked horseshoe.

The tiles are an emptied graph of my life:
I finally have to flush and take a stand,
I must peel myself from this cracked horseshoe.
I finger the whitewashed words and clear my throat.

I finally have to flush and take a stand!
As he palms a thin red liquid from the dispenser,
I finger the whitewashed words and clear my throat.
The chairman is washing his dirty hands again.

The All-Dog Siren Choir

Their ears can smell trouble coming
miles away, its painful scent:

even the faintest ambulance
triggers unconditional keening

for the firestruck and crimeridden,
for all the sick and injured and dead,

a ghastly polyphonic sobbing
shocking our neighborhood's sober air

with the hackle-raising grief
of blind cockers, half-cocked dachsunds,

sentimental crapulous Irish tenors,
the labs' black baritone.

Under their hysterical blues
the siren's orchestra builds to crescendo

and flashes by, but the mournful dogs
continue to make lamentation,

answering wail for wail for wail for wail
long after Emergency has passed,

their grief ludicrous to the cats
sharpening their claws, staying out of it,

but pleasing somehow to the tone-deaf angels
and their dyslexic god.

November 22, 1963

Friday afternoon, Mrs. Franklin's fourth-grade class
sunk in a pre-weekend waking nap, our post-lunch slump,
cloudy windows cracked, hallway quiet, nothing happening,

when suddenly the loudspeaker crackles and our principal,
instead of making an announcement about the library
or summoning one of us to the office, simply says,

"The president has been shot" and puts the microphone
against the crackly radio, the broadcast from Dallas,
and lets it run until school is out ninety minutes later

and the president is dead, and we all have stiff necks
from looking up at the words as they fell from the box,
through the ripped speaker cloth, through the static air,

and that weekend we all watch as a man in a black suit
shoots a man in a black sweater who had shot our president
as he rode in a limousine on that endless Friday afternoon.

Address Book

It looks like an overcensored document,
a welter of blistering horizontals

signifying death, divorce, disaster,
the steady migration of affection.

Like a rueful recording angel,
I continue the obliteration,
striking every backslider
from this memorial to correspondence:

people I have loved and touched, now remote,
people whose mere return address could once delight me,
people who outgrew letters and cards, or never quite
    grew into them,
people always too busy to write or call,
people I shared a drink with somewhere,
people who only gave me their office addresses,
people I have never even seen,
people who wouldn't have to strike my name from their
    old address books,
people with one unlikely thing in common:

me.

I knew a guy once who, when depressed,
would take out his pocket address book
and make a list of all those people
he might describe as friends. Next,
he's cross out all the people on the list
he didn't consider *good* friends. Finally,
he'd eliminate the people he couldn't call
really good friends, those who would gladly
lay down their life or money for him.

And end without a single name unstruck,
an address book bristling with enemies.

———————

Paranoid, sure; but who can't understand
his chronic disappointment with the world,
that angry helpless grief for all the connections

lost, lapsed, botched, lingering in the mind
like a dim constellation of scars?

———————

There's my mother's name, cauterized
by three deep lines, isolating
my late father from his surname,
as if I could still mail him a letter.

There's an old girlfriend, violently cancelled.

There's a famous poet I wrote once, hoping for—
what? a word that would change my life somehow?

There's a former student who wrote me once,
mistaking me for a famous poet.

And there's my gentle friend, whose cells
will soon devour the stories he should have told,
blotting his name from the page.

———————

To *address* is to straighten,
to direct oneself toward something,

which is why this old book
is such a rough and frustrating draft,

each phrase and phase perpetually revised,
a palimpsest of insertion and deletion.

———————

I review this census of loss
one last time, like a nightmare
in which, for some mysterious reason,

every student has dropped my course,
leaving only my own name unexpunged
at the top of the class roll.

I transfer the names of the elect,
the faithful and the lucky ones,
into a trim new address book,
each one smaller than the last.

The pen says its ink is permanent,
but we all know better.

Ice Cube

Not really a cube at all
but an anvil floating upside-down in his glass,

a clapper in the bell of his tumbler,
its clink a familiar music they play all evening
like cows coming home.

Crystal briquet lit by his lukewarm drink.

An island whose shores
constantly shrink toward a frozen core,

the iris of the coldest eye staring him down.

Domestic physics:
a starburst of gases inside a solid
suspended in a succession of liquid media,
all moving toward equilibrium

until he spoils everything with his thirst again,
his careless mouth.

Cancer

Now when they touch, she scans his skin
for signs of impending disaster,

for spots or moles that seem to be rising
as part of an odd constellation

of negative stars whose appetite might
one day devour his body

increasingly crowded with ominous mistakes,
with marks redeemed by no mythology.

The Story

It's how the book glows on his pillow in the intimate lamplight
as she slips into bed, fresh sheets nuzzling her body
mollified by a leisurely bath:

it's how her puckered hands slowly lift it from his place
to her face, tenderly breaking it as she inhales
the musk of new paper and ink:

it's how the bed sighs as she sinks to a comfortable position,
the title page kissing her fingers, the first line
gazing deep into her dilated eyes:

it's how she's instantly lost in the story and lost to him
lurking in the hall's tall bookish shadows,
listening to the pages whisper:

it's how she reads till she falls asleep clutching the book,
as if she could keep reading through closed lids
or deeply breathe the words' oxygen:

it's how he finally tiptoes in and dogears the unfinished page
and pulls the cover up to her untouchable neck
and squeezes the light into silence

and paces the maze of the house like a jealous adjective
looking all night long for its unfaithful noun,
for a chance to get back in the story.

The Bat

Slightly ahead of cue, the nightmare bat
makes a quiet entrance as the man and woman
yawn off to bed: they cover their heads
and fall to the floor swearing and shouting
while this scrap of animated darkness
continues its circulation of the house
they'd thought so secure.
                            But now the house
has a black corpuscle in its veins, a bat
swimming efficient laps from one darkness
to another. Each time it appears, the woman
brandishes her dangerous pillow, shouting
Where did it come from? as the shadow heads
back into the hall.
                    They swaddle their heads
with cast-off clothes. The adrenalized house
is a silent horror movie filled with shouting
they can't hear: a German expressionist bat
thirsty for the blood of a married woman
won't quit haunting their mortgaged darkness
until a sacrifice is made!
                        This darkness,
the man thinks, *it must be a sign.* He heads
for the light switch, crawling; the woman
opens the front and back doors of the house,
which is having a bad dream about a bat
falling down the chimney, a couple shouting
at it and each other,

       and a house shouting
itself awake, suffocating in darkness.
Ready? the man calls to her, as the bat
continues to skate the ice over their heads
like a burglar taking inventory of the house,
taking his time, taking everything. The woman
grows used to it:
              the bat seems like a woman
looking for a way out, her calm shouting
functional—a way of escaping the house.
The man is a distant noise, the darkness
part of a brittle puzzle between their heads.
It is the missing piece, the shape of a bat.

Has the woman vanished, like the sooty bat?
The man is shouting to an emptied house.
The darkness has many wings and many heads.

The Falls

This is the creek that feeds the falls.
    There is the other side.
Here are the slippery stepping stones
    where some have died—

a redneck on a whiskey dare,
    a scout who lost his head,
a couple of midnight lovers fresh
    from their mossy bed.

The creek is cold but not too deep,
    though deep enough to drown.
You can savor its mortal aftertaste
    at any tap in town,

at any tap in any town
    from here to the bitter sea.
There's nothing for you on the other side.
    Stay here with me.

V

Perpetual

The gaunt woman on her ancient bike
circles our streets in any weather,
a dark leitmotif in the local opera,
never sprinting, never coasting, never
resting her bony body on the saddle,
her mask-like face fixed in a grimace
that could be a smile, it's hard to tell
because she never turns or pauses or stops,
she has been riding this bicycle so long
her arms are handlebars, her legs are part
of the pedals spinning the silent chain
that never rusts because she never quits
engaging it, a fabulous creature part woman
part machine, refining itself into nothing.

The Roof Men

may be drunk, or stoned. They stand
atop the library like an indolent frieze,
or loll on cornice, chimney pot, and parapet.
The bell tower is their time clock, its hands

big as God's. They stir caldrons of tar
that smell like cancer, smoke cigarettes
and stir, spit comets into the alumni garden
aiming for Cupid, whistle at the coeds far

below, deaf to their influence on heaven.
One man works while a dozen supervise
him, and campus, and the sky ready to leak,
remote as their next check or the weekend.

The roof men cough, laugh, fake a fight,
and stir tar so black it seems composed
of all the letters in all the books below,
drawn to their broth like moths to final light.

Performance

The artist with all the words
inked on the back of her hand
keeps pausing in her monologue

to check them, as if their code
were a crib sheet for the test
of where she should go next

and what she should say, her lips
flaring as she tries to decipher
the dark side of her lifeline,

wondering why she put these words
in this order, and why the alphabet
lines up ABC, and why in hell

God has started speaking to her
in Korean, should she pray or sing
in her quivery alto, it's scary

watching her decide what to do,
she could damage herself right here
in front of everybody, but instead

she's just taking off her clothes
and, look, words have been hidden
everywhere, her body is a text

scripted in many different hands,
it's a journal written and written
over and over, it's a cryptograph

of love letters no one can read
but her, she's even been tattooed
inside, with tiny blue sutures,

that's the story she could tell
if she'd close those wide wide eyes
and calm that flickering tongue:

there is nowhere words are not.

Linville Caverns

Our guide's a walking stalagmite, a pale kid
with his certificate in Creative Geology.
He swipes a flashlight at nicknamed formations—
Franciscan Monk, Taco Meat, The Capitol Dome.
We can't see a thing, so we make up our own:
Revival Preacher, Indigestion, The Senator at Play.

He infects the mountain's sinus with his drone:
the cave-stream trout that are "98 percent blind,"
the fate of the Union and Confederate deserters
who hid in this chilly hell during the War,
the star-crossed Linville Lovers . . . We gasp
with laughter as he hurtles us along, passing

the other shivering tour groups, squeezing
deeper and deeper into the dripping caverns.
"Please don't touch the formations," he warns.
"There are salts and oils on the human skin:
if you touch them, they'll stop growing forever."
"Don't touch," we echo. "Human skin. Forever."

Suddenly we're alone, wedged in a cul-de-sac.
"Have you ever experienced Total Darkness?" he asks,
then hits the lights and leaves us suffocating
there in the black too absolute for metaphor.
And then we hear a distant voice, a curse:
"You might go blind, but you'll go crazy first."

Shoulder

So much smoother than its rough cousins,
those evolutionary throwbacks, Elbow and Knee.

Should is its foundation, conditional futurity.
I should very much like to kiss her shoulder.

Posing for pictures, we reach for shoulders.
Their invisible epaulets tickle our palms.

The shoulder itself is never really cold.
An aromatic shadow incubates beneath it.

Somebody pruned it ruthlessly, long ago:
it blossomed inward, musculature and skeleton.

Leonardo understood how the shoulder
will always ache for its phantom wing.

It is the fulfillment of an empty hand.
It is the beginning or the end of something.

Pas de Deux

Sleep is our long dark dance.
   All night we turn
with a grace impossible by day,
    feeling for each other

like parts of a single body:
   under the blank sheet
hands know where to find hands,
    feet stretch for feet,

we fill the bed's familiar stage
  and disappear
deep into our mirrored breath,
    delivered from the fear

of a mattress left half-empty,
  of having to learn
that difficult long dark dance
    without a partner.

When I Read to My Son

he instinctively places his hand
on my wrist, a feathery cuff

confirming the sluggish pace
of a world that is already

disappearing with his breath.
Sometimes I want to stop, close

the book and say, Blink, breathe,
don't believe anything, especially

words, so utterly! But sometimes
I convince myself that this therapy

will save his life. And so I say
nothing except the imperfect story

somebody else wrote, and we sit
for hours at this strange transfusion

of words, and his touch is steady
as a blind boy guiding his guide.

My Aunt Smokes Another Lucky

She slips it out of its leatherette case,
an immaculate cartridge
she clenches between the red bow of her lips
while flicking her butane lighter,
sucking deeply until the tip
starts to crackle and glow like a fuse.

She snaps the lighter shut and blows smoke
through pursed lips over her shoulder,
lifting the Lucky between two rednail fingers
like somebody about to take an oath,
her hand's glamorous gesture
echoing the pale curve of her cheek.

She smokes her way through another story,
punctuates it with the Lucky
she keeps sharp with crisp drags and raps
into the Everglades souvenir ashtray.
She squints at her cigarette:
one bitter puff and she wrings its neck

in the overflowing nest of ashes,
the lipstick on its butt so alluring
that when I start smoking candy cigarettes
I put the lit end in my mouth
and everybody laughs, especially my aunt,
smoke haunting her head like ghosts of family.

Pearly Gates

Sweet Aunt Thelma, coaxing me
to eat spoonfuls of mushy food,
sings her little off-key song:
Open up those pearly gates!

I watch the fishy silver dance
of spoon in air, the golden flash
of molars in her model mouth,
then laugh, and open up, and eat.

Years later, bored together
in the lugubrious backseat
on a family drive to Florida,
I say to her, *Let's play dentist!*

and reach to tug on her front teeth
and find myself holding the slick
pink roof of my Aunt Thelma's mouth,
kernels of teeth in a perfect arc.

I gasp as if bitten, then I gag,
dropping her half-smile on the floor,
terrified by her altered laugh
filling the cavity of the car

and the rotten mouth of Georgia
swallowing us as we head south
and the hungry sky behind the sky
with its unreachable pearly clouds.

Colander

Upside down, a holy helmet
crowning my son's impressionable head,
its feet fierce horns.

A planetarium dome
sieving light in ideal patterns.

On its feet, an altar vessel,
six stars surrounding a larger seventh
through which water falls

and billows like the breath of God
from a battered censer.

A mask of sweet ether
my blinded mother lifted to her face
over the still-steaming sink.

Recipes

Concentrated manuscripts
copied out at kitchen tables after good meals
and proofread for quantity and degree,

they were handed down
from grandmother to mother to daughter,
from sister to sister, from friend to hungry friend,

pages from the never-finished history of appetite
written in a range of styles
but always in the familiar imperative.

The best ones were stained with their own ingredients.
You could find them in cookbooks or boxes
or (as with my mother) in a drawer

stuffed full as a Thanksgiving turkey
with index cards, sheets from notepads and notebooks,
whatever paper was available

blue with her impatient arthritic cursive—
flavors I still remember
when I find her favorite recipes in an old envelope.

They are receipts for some unaccountable hunger.
They are prescriptions that might yet cure.
They are something given, and received:

take, eat.